# Ink Tracing Book

# Introduction to Tracing

Have you ever admired intricate patterns and wondered how someone could create such perfect lines? Do you want to draw but don't know where to start? Or are you looking for a way to calm your mind and relax through art? If so, "Ink Tracing Book" is for you!

Tracing is one of the simplest yet most effective methods for improving drawing skills. It involves following existing lines, helping you develop better hand control, precision, and confidence with your pen or marker. More than just a technical exercise, it's also a wonderful way to relax—rhythmic hand movements and the focus required to trace each shape allow you to escape daily stress and enter a state of creative flow.

This book is designed to help you enjoy tracing, whether you are a beginner exploring the basics of line work or an artist looking for inspiration to refine your skills. Each pattern in this book has been carefully prepared with a light, 20% opacity, making it easy for you to follow the lines and enhance them with your own ink strokes.

## How to Use This Book?

### Choose Your Drawing Tool

You can use a variety of tools for tracing—fine liners, ballpoint pens, markers, or even brush pens with ink. For clean, crisp lines, we recommend fine-tipped pens or gel pens.

### Find a Comfortable Position

Make sure you have a comfortable workspace. Tracing requires precision, so ensure you have proper hand support and good lighting.

### Start with Light Strokes

At first, don't press too hard. Let your hand flow naturally over the lines, allowing for smooth and effortless movement.

### Experiment with Styles

You can follow the lines exactly or add your own twist—varying line thickness, adding decorative elements, or combining patterns in new ways.

### Focus on the Process

Perfection is not the goal. Tracing is about mindfulness and creativity. Allow yourself to explore and enjoy each stroke of the pen.

Each left-hand page of this book contains inspirational tips and guidance to help you develop your tracing skills and make the most of this technique. Treat this book as a space for experimentation and discovery, embracing the joy of drawing.

Now, there's only one thing left to do—pick up your pen and let the lines guide you into the world of creative exploration!

Use slow, controlled movements for smooth lines

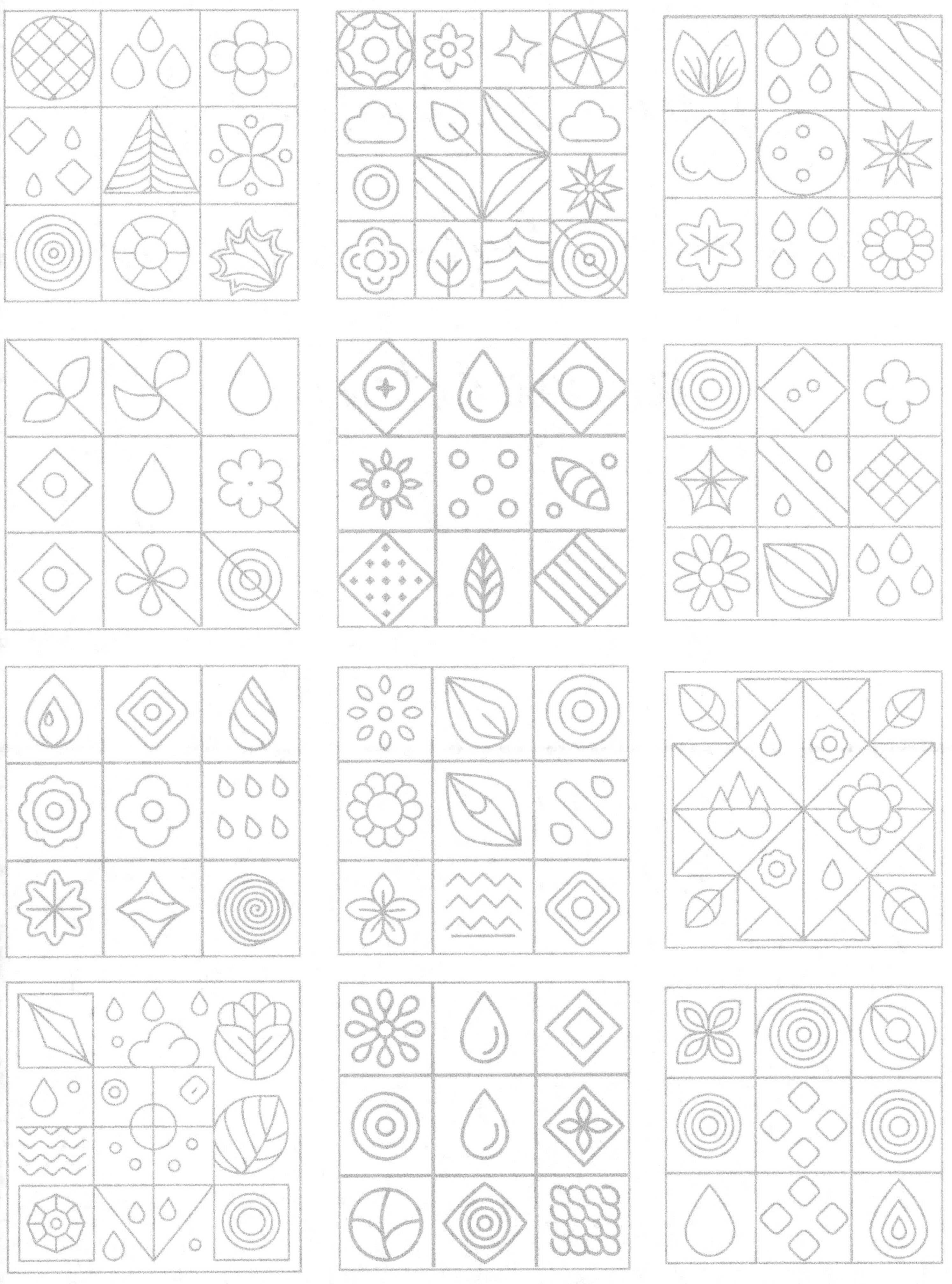

Start with light pressure, then darken as needed.

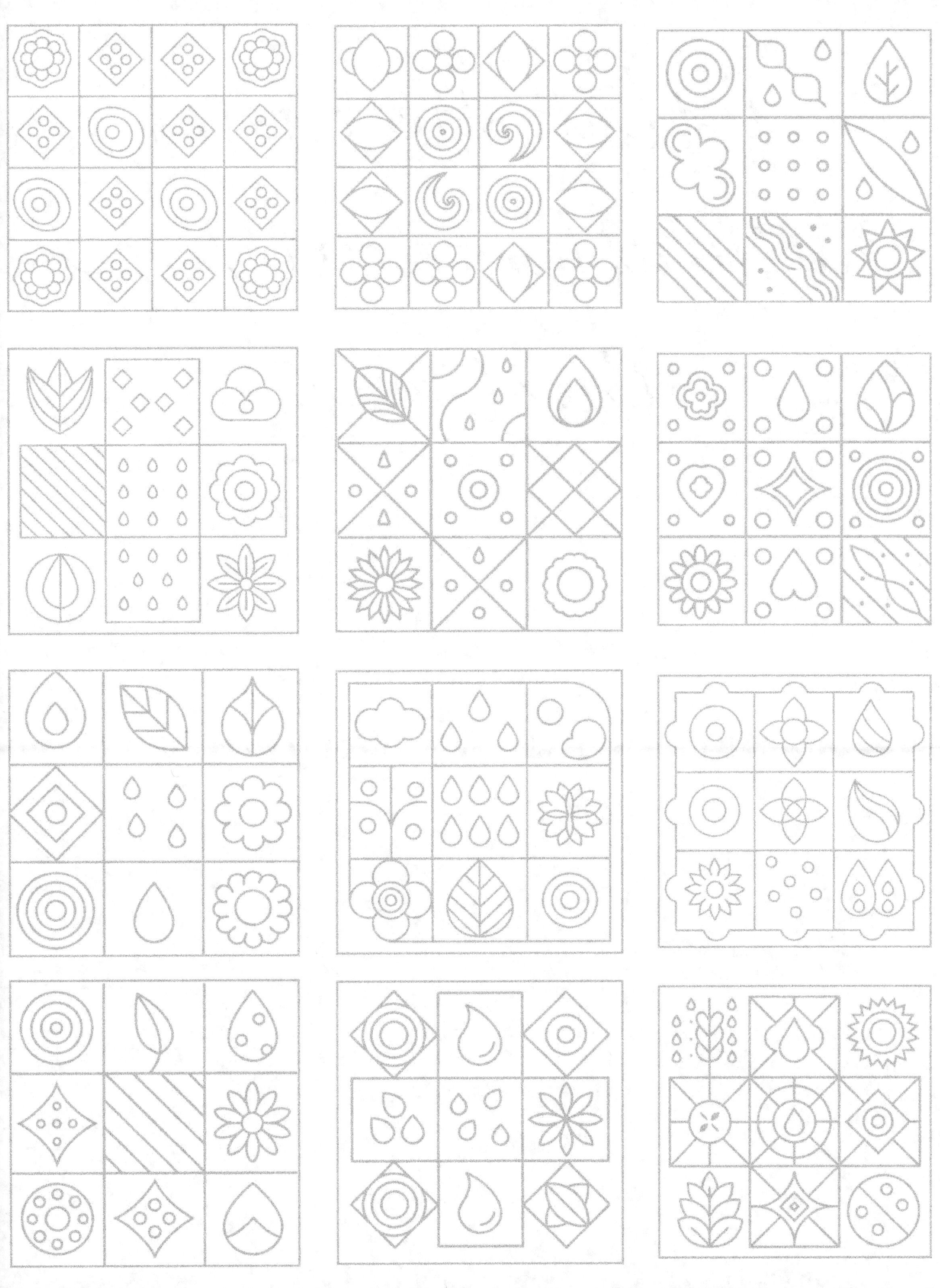

Follow the curves naturally—don't force the lines.

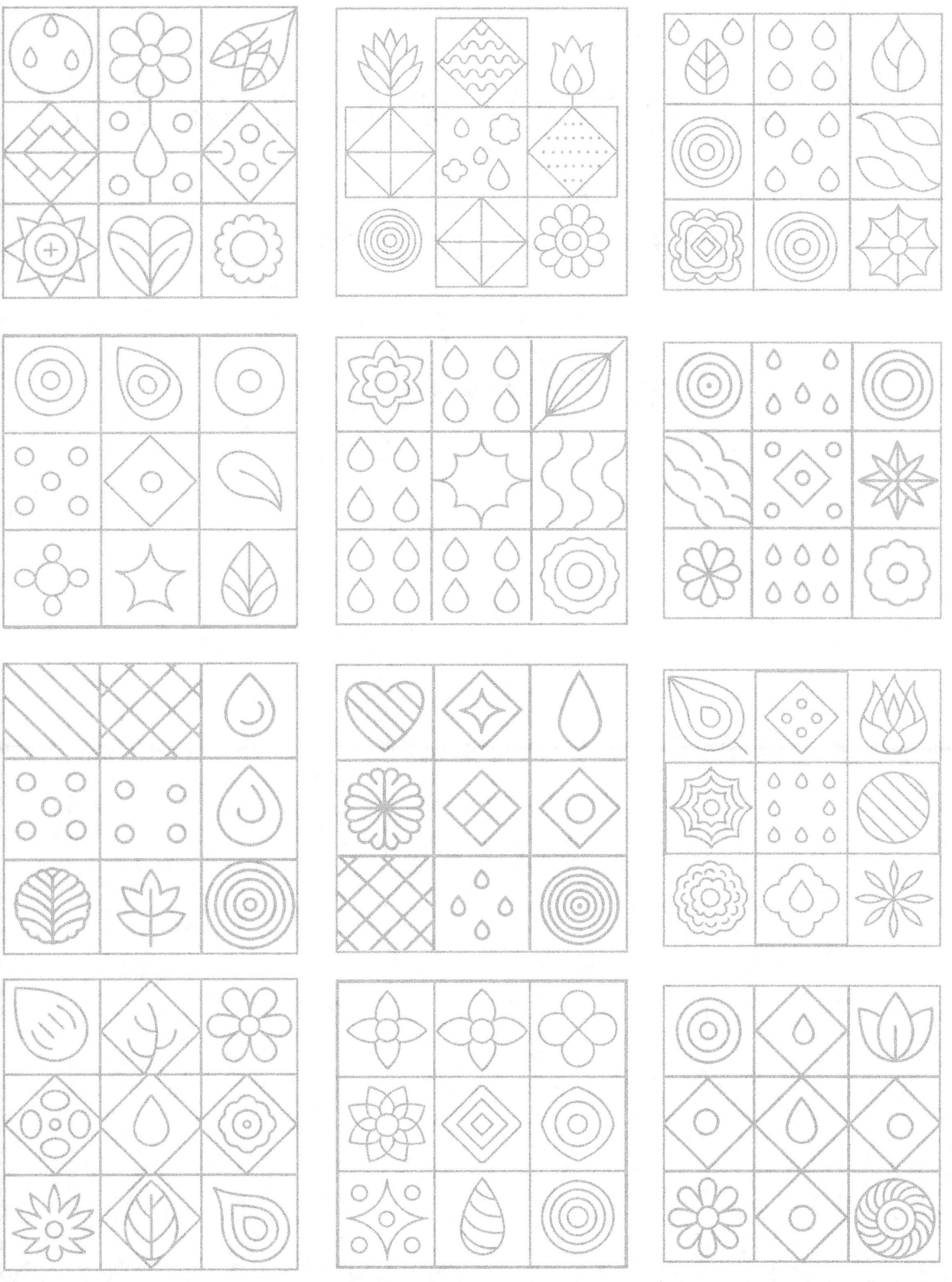

Maintain a consistent hand position for stability.

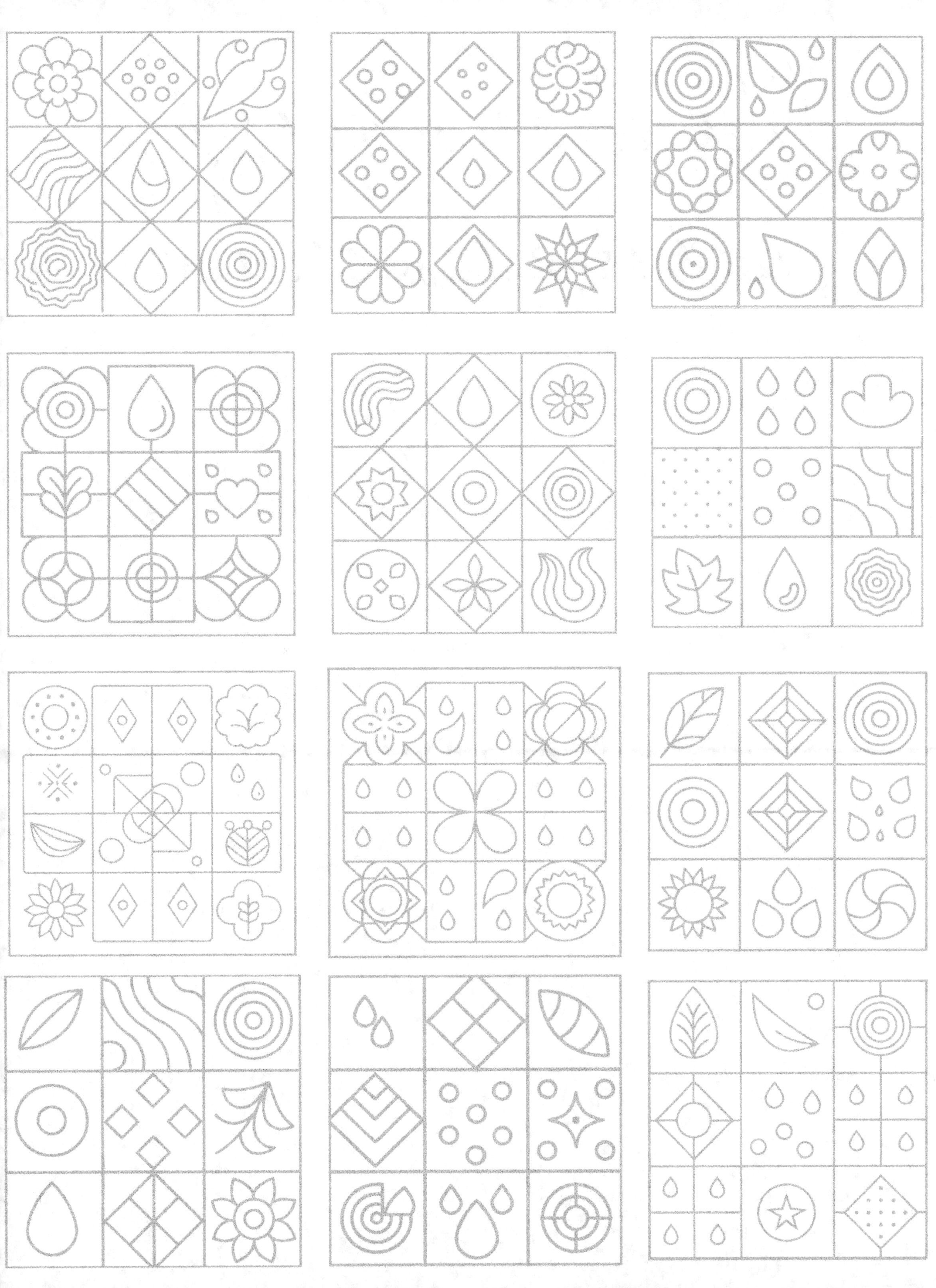

Use short strokes for detailed sections.

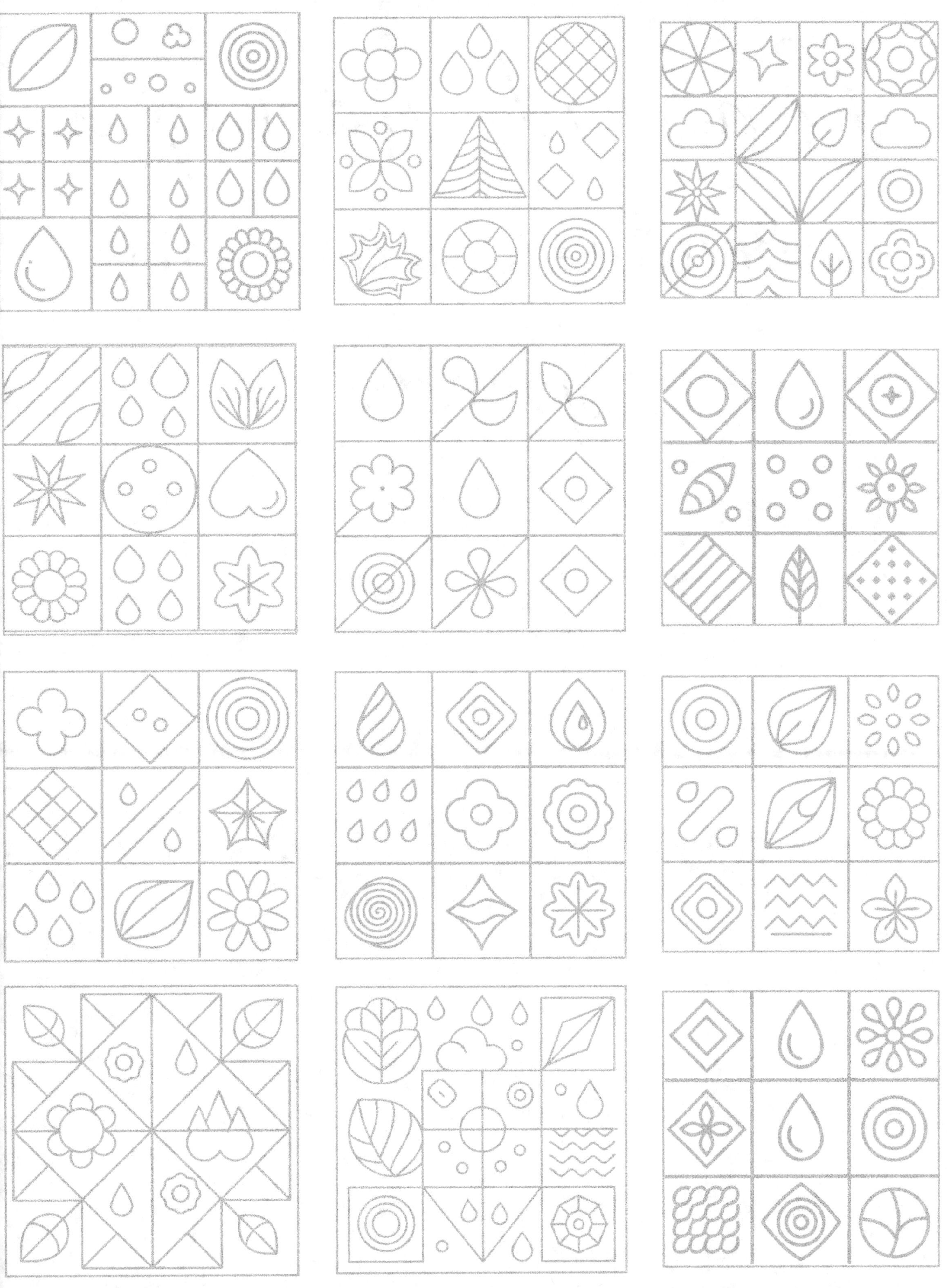

Don't rush-tracing is about precision, not speed.

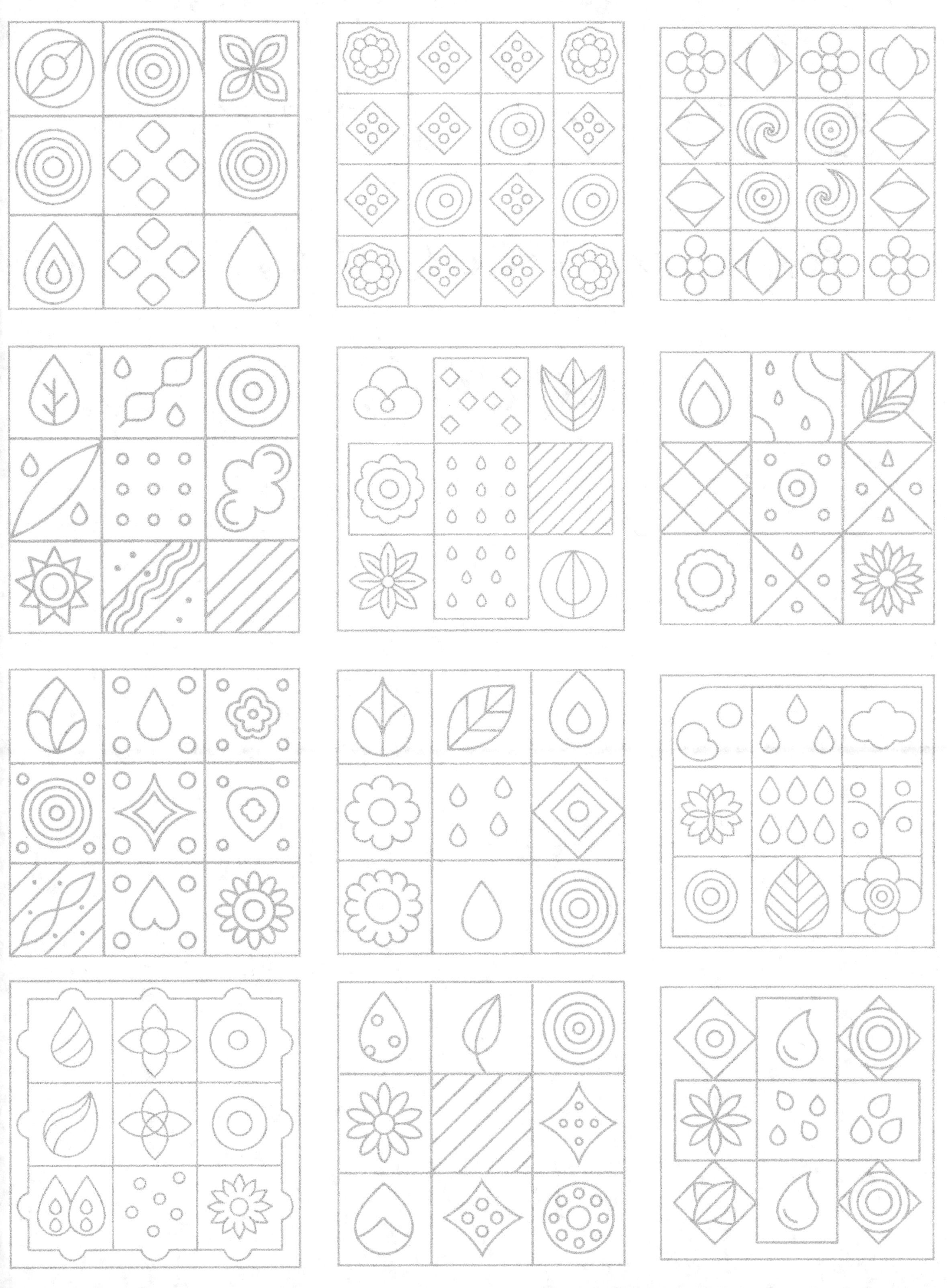

Don't rush—tracing is about precision, not speed.

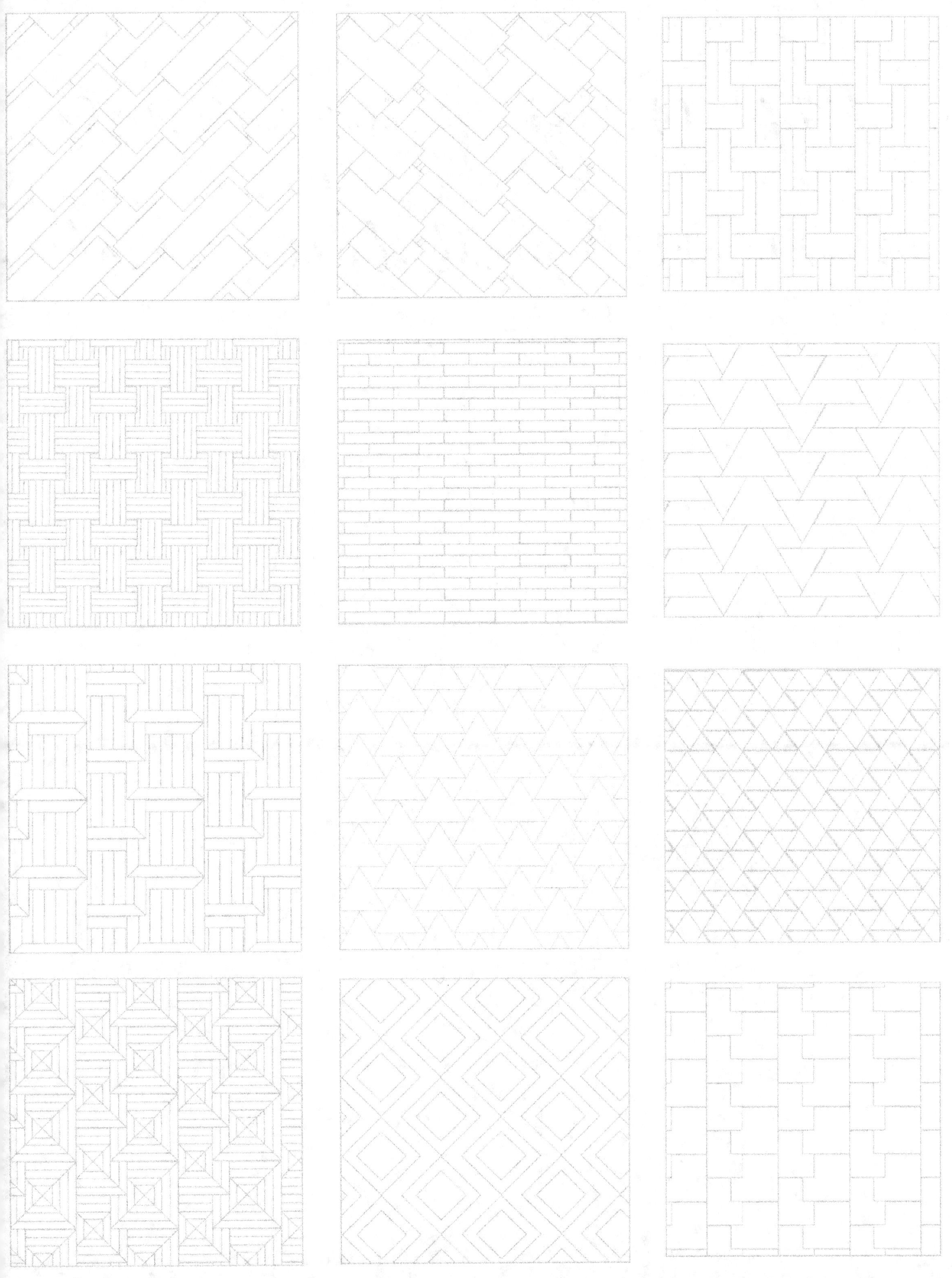

Try using your entire arm, not just the wrist.

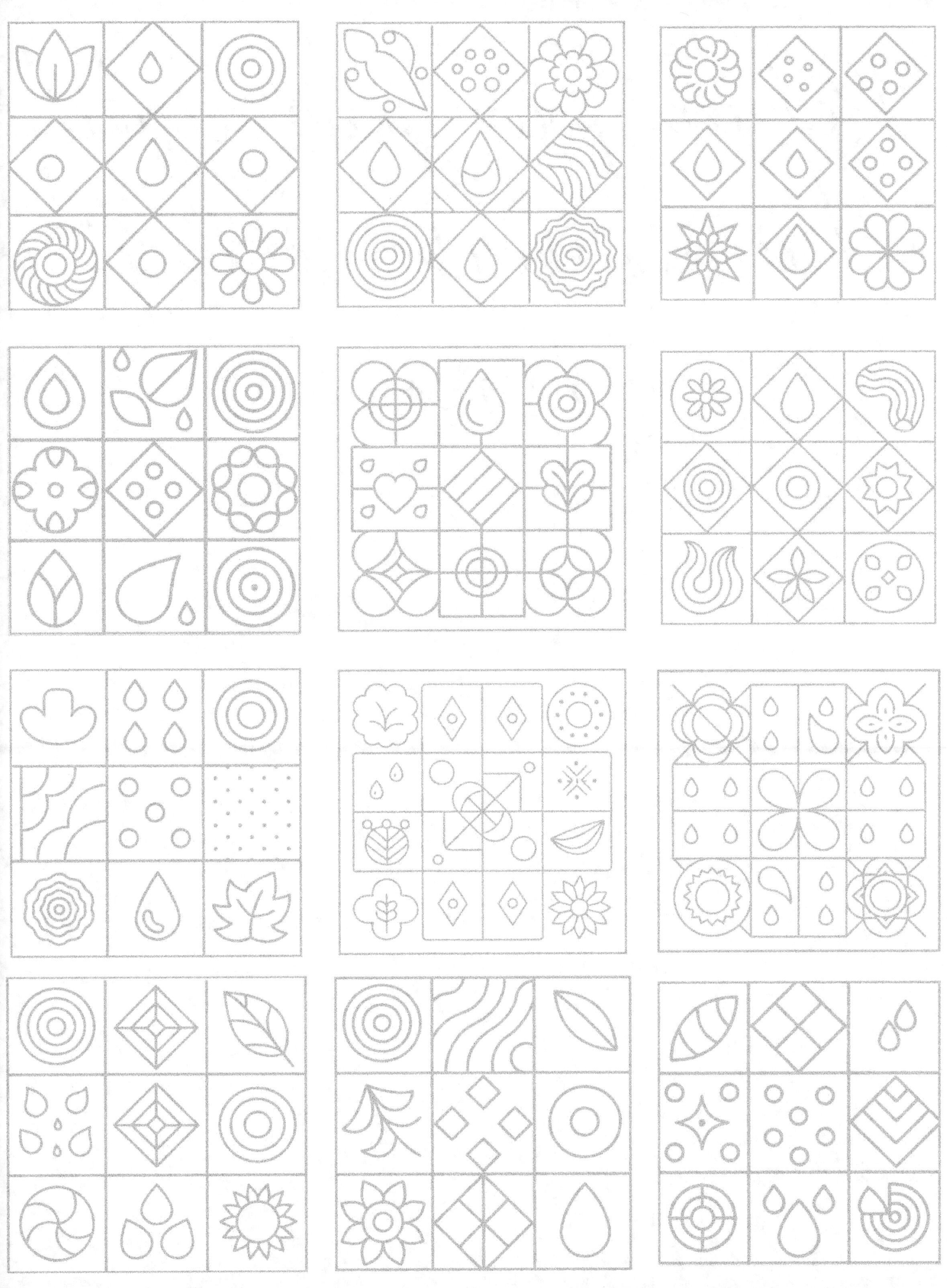

Relax your grip—tight hands make shaky lines.

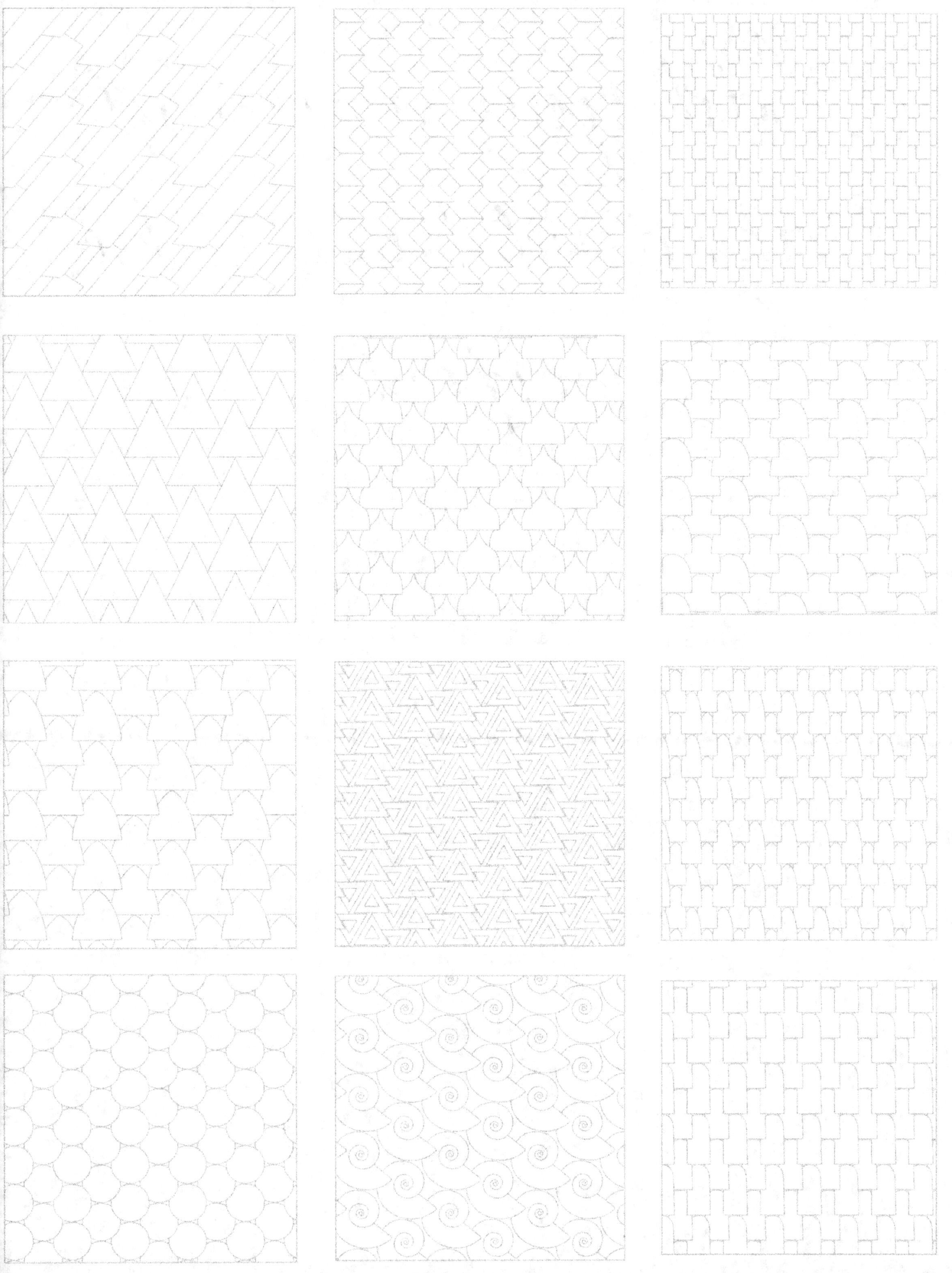

Add your own twist—lines don't have to be perfect.

After tracing, try embellishing with extra details.

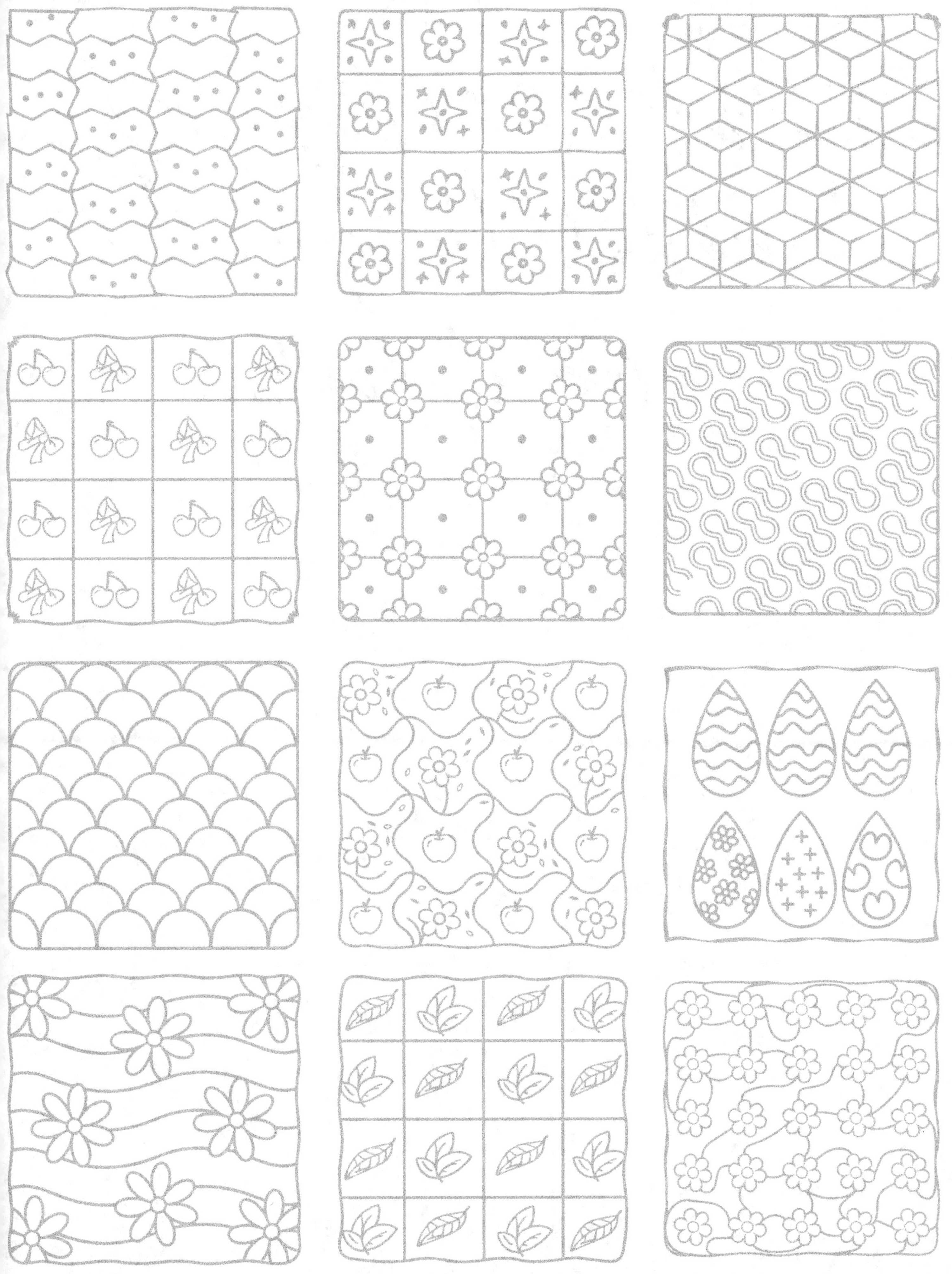

After tracing, try embellishing with extra details.

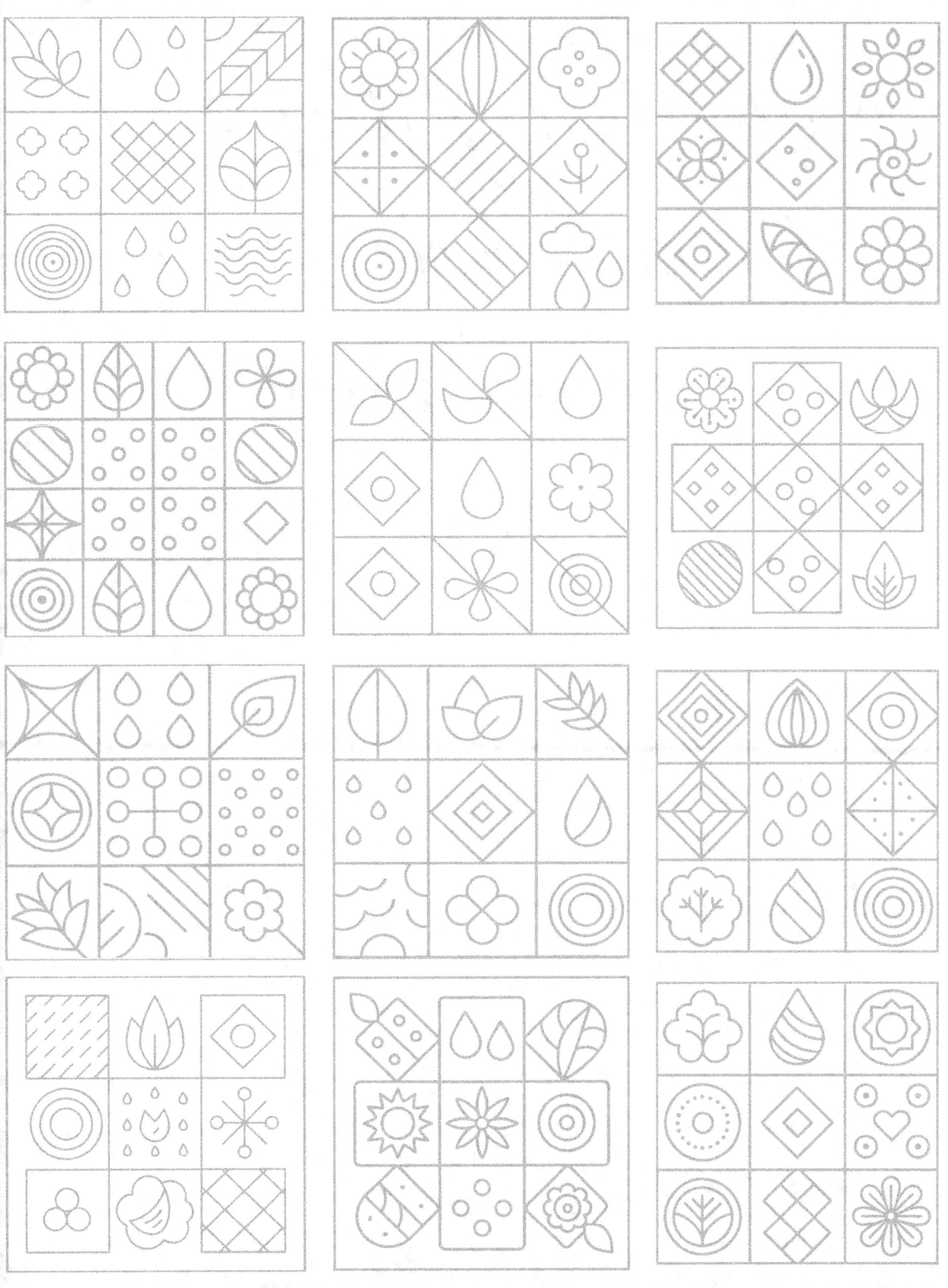

Outline lightly first, then go bold on a second pass.

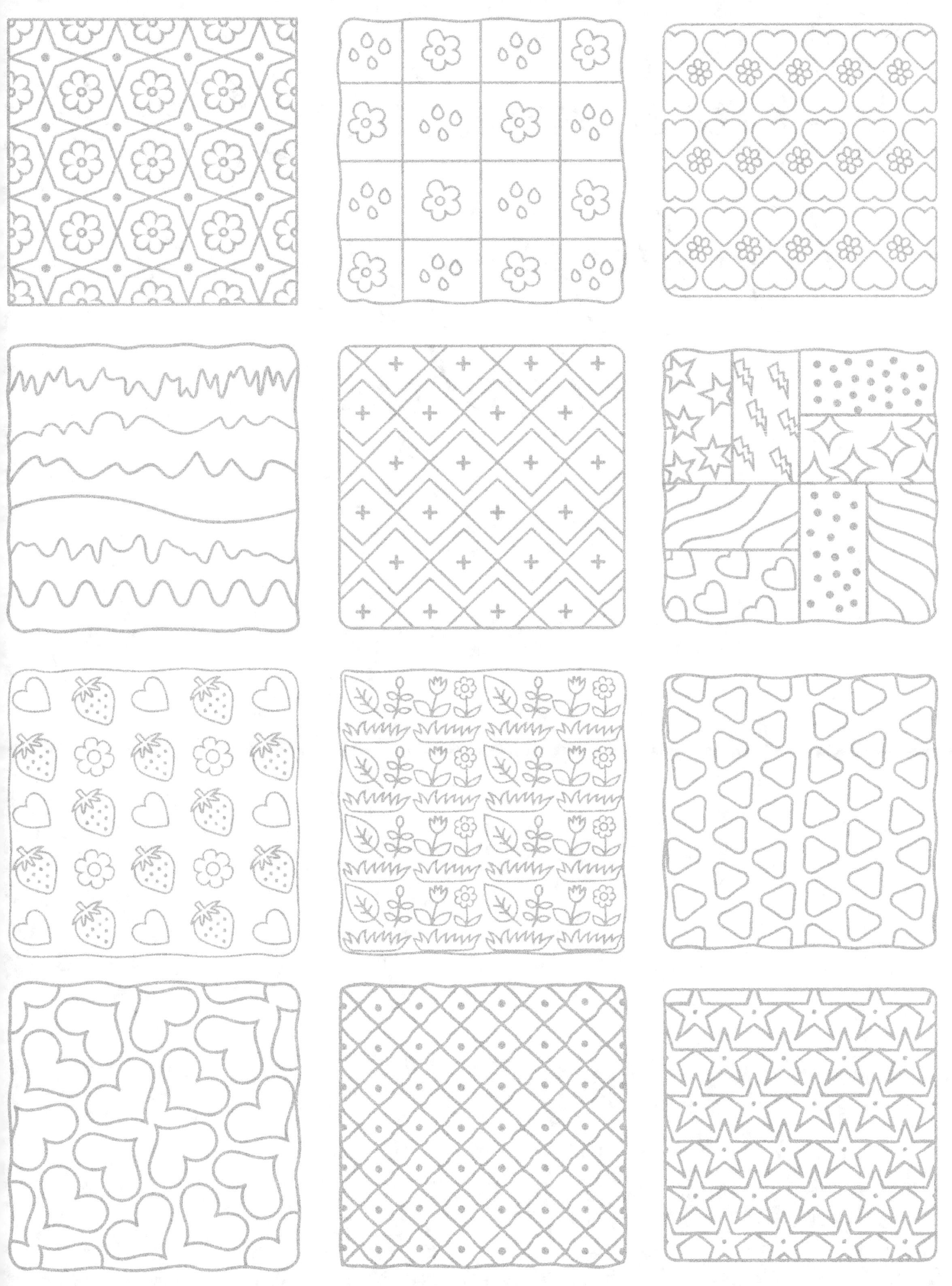

Create shadow effects by layering lines closely.

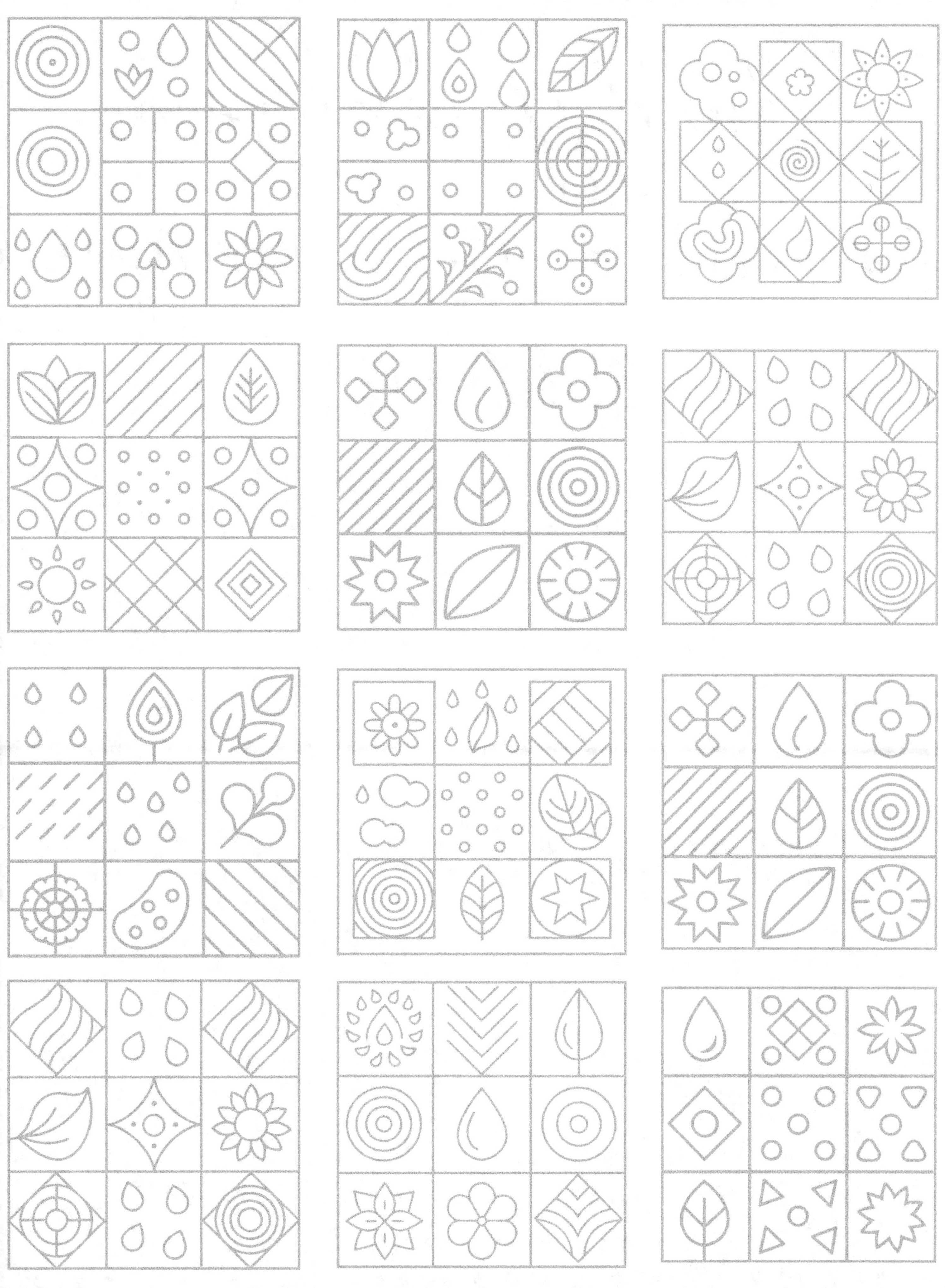

Use different pen types to explore unique textures.

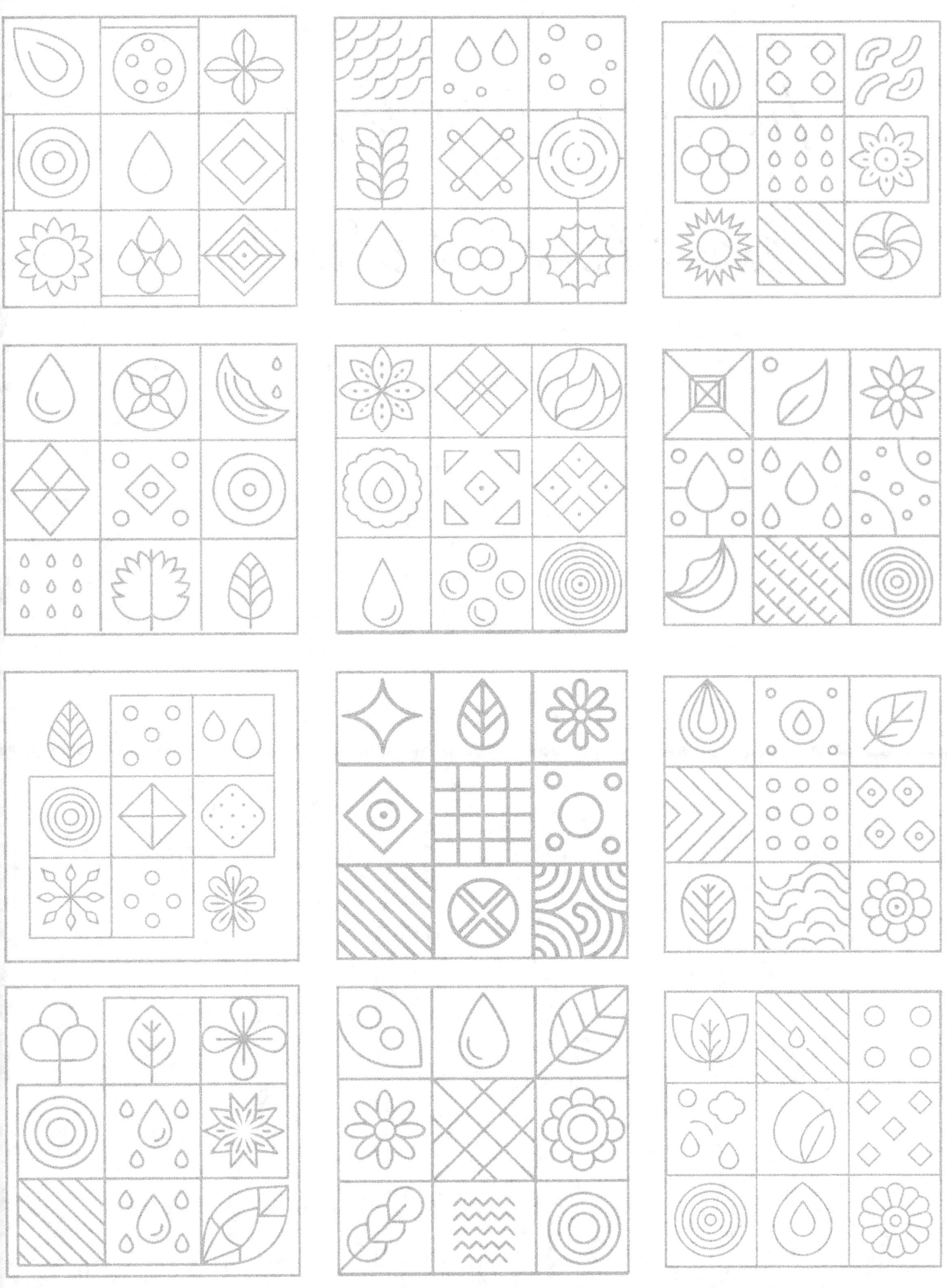

# Turn mistakes into creative details!

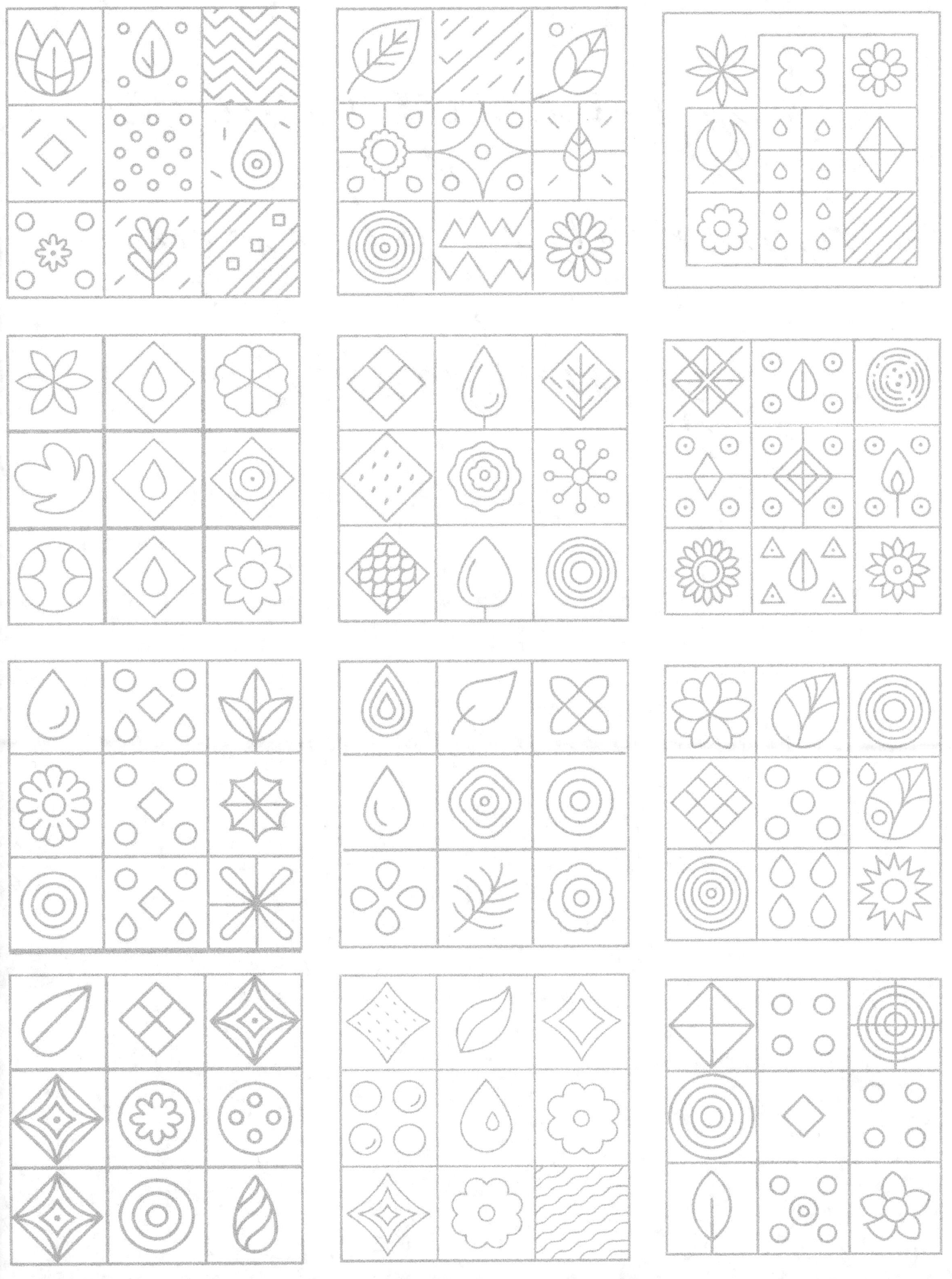

Try tracing upside down-it challenges your brain!

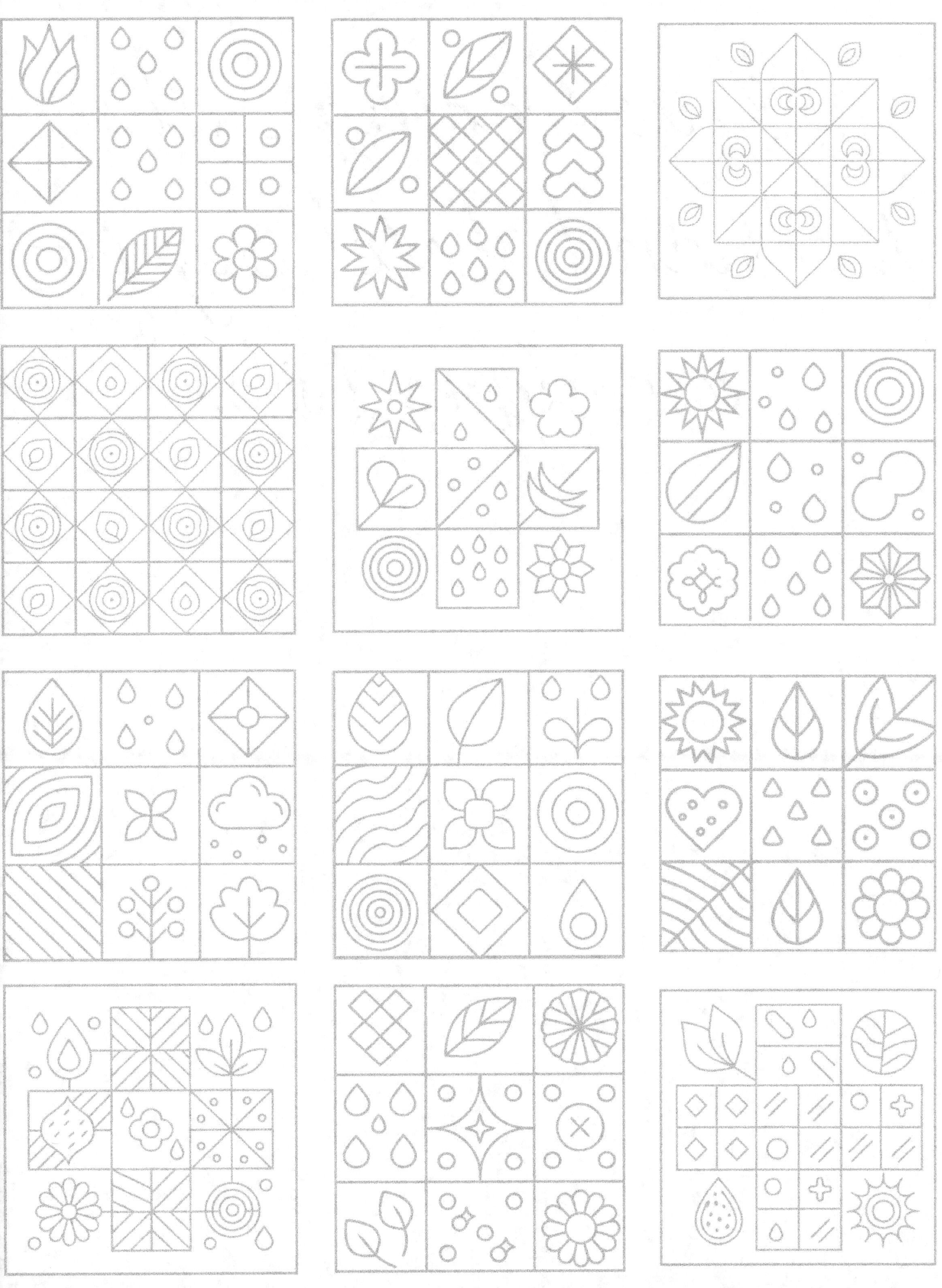

Mix tracing with freehand sketching for a unique look.

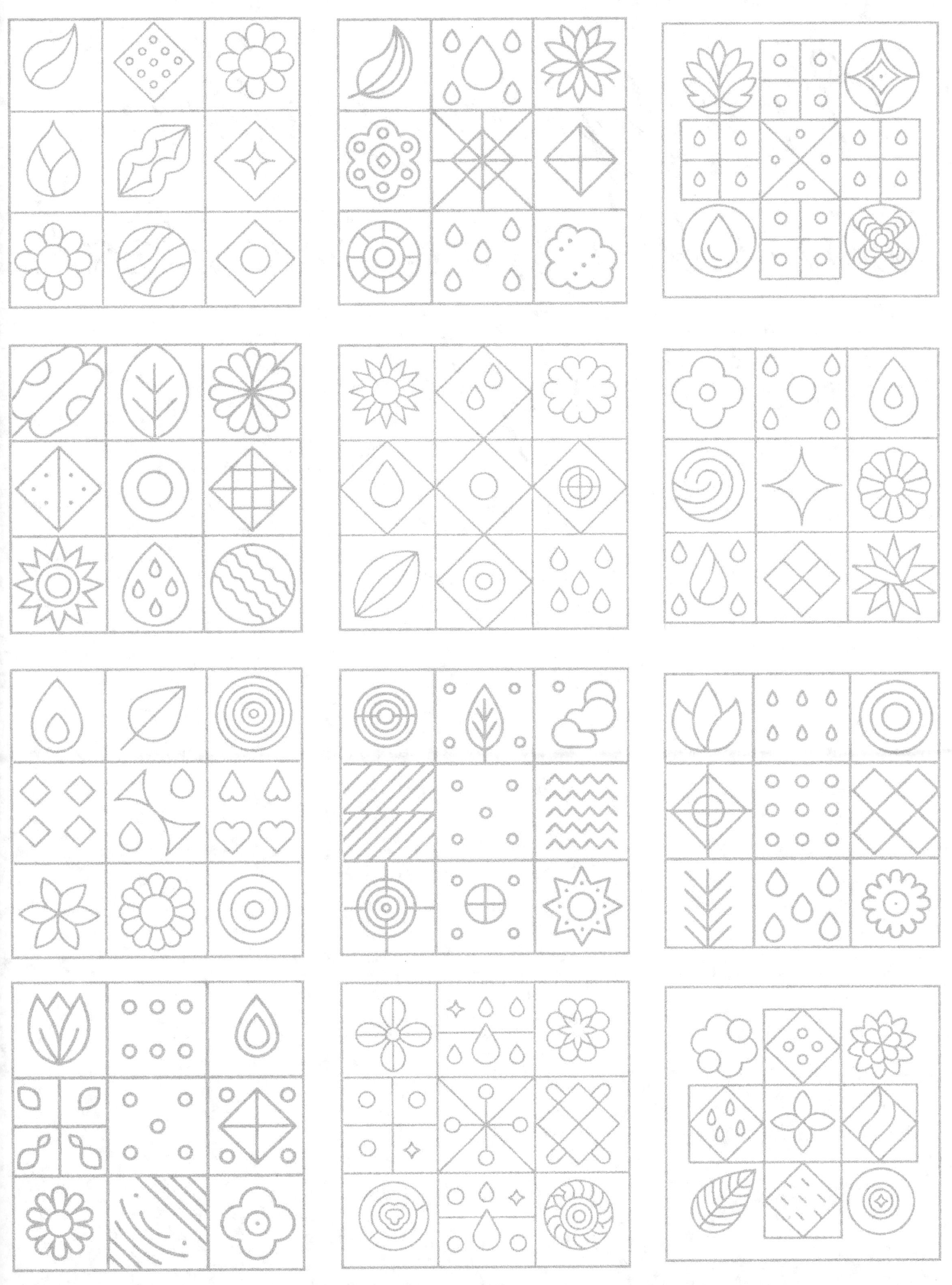

Modify the patterns
to match your personal
style.

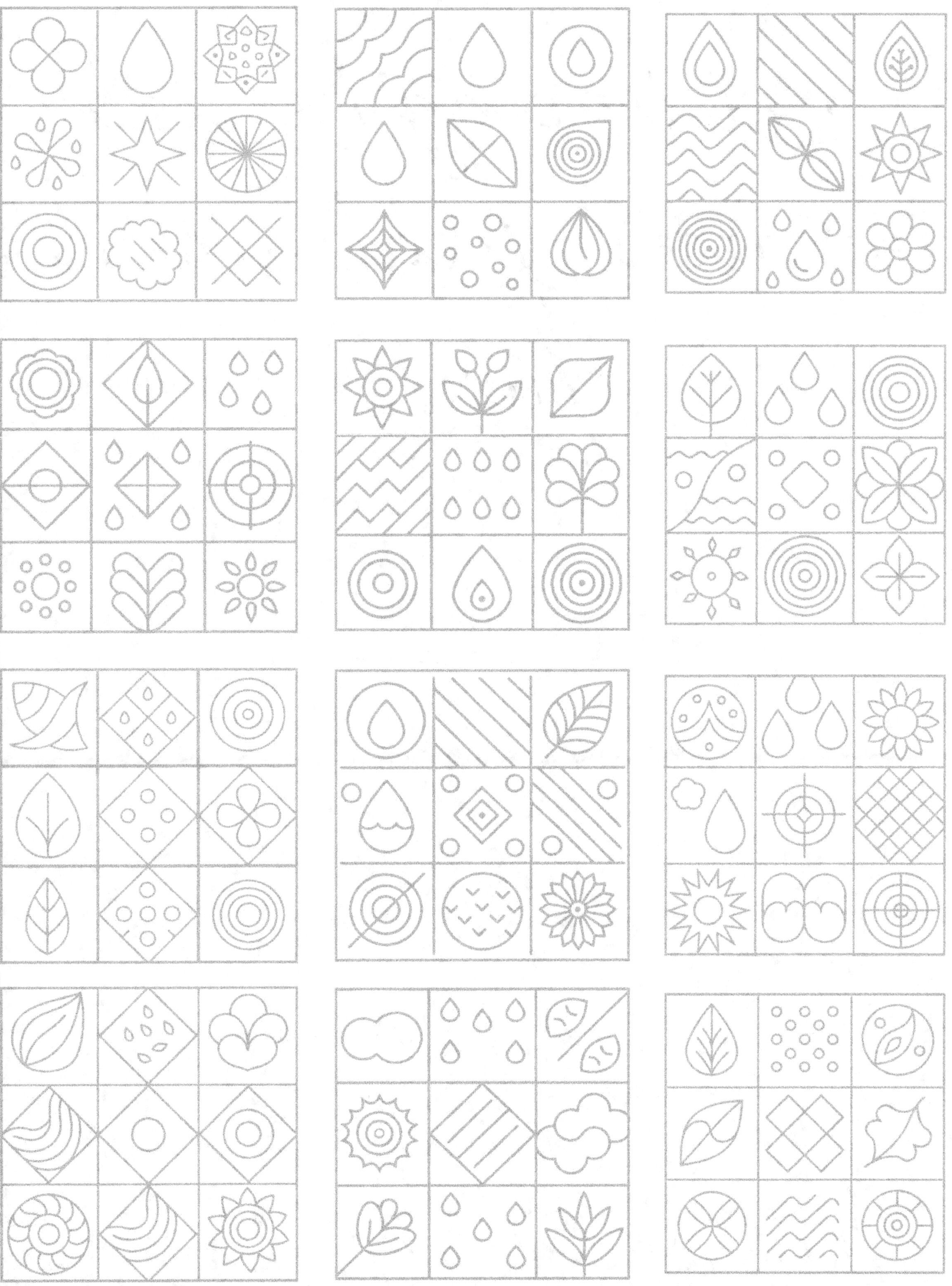

Let tracing be your moment of calm and focus.

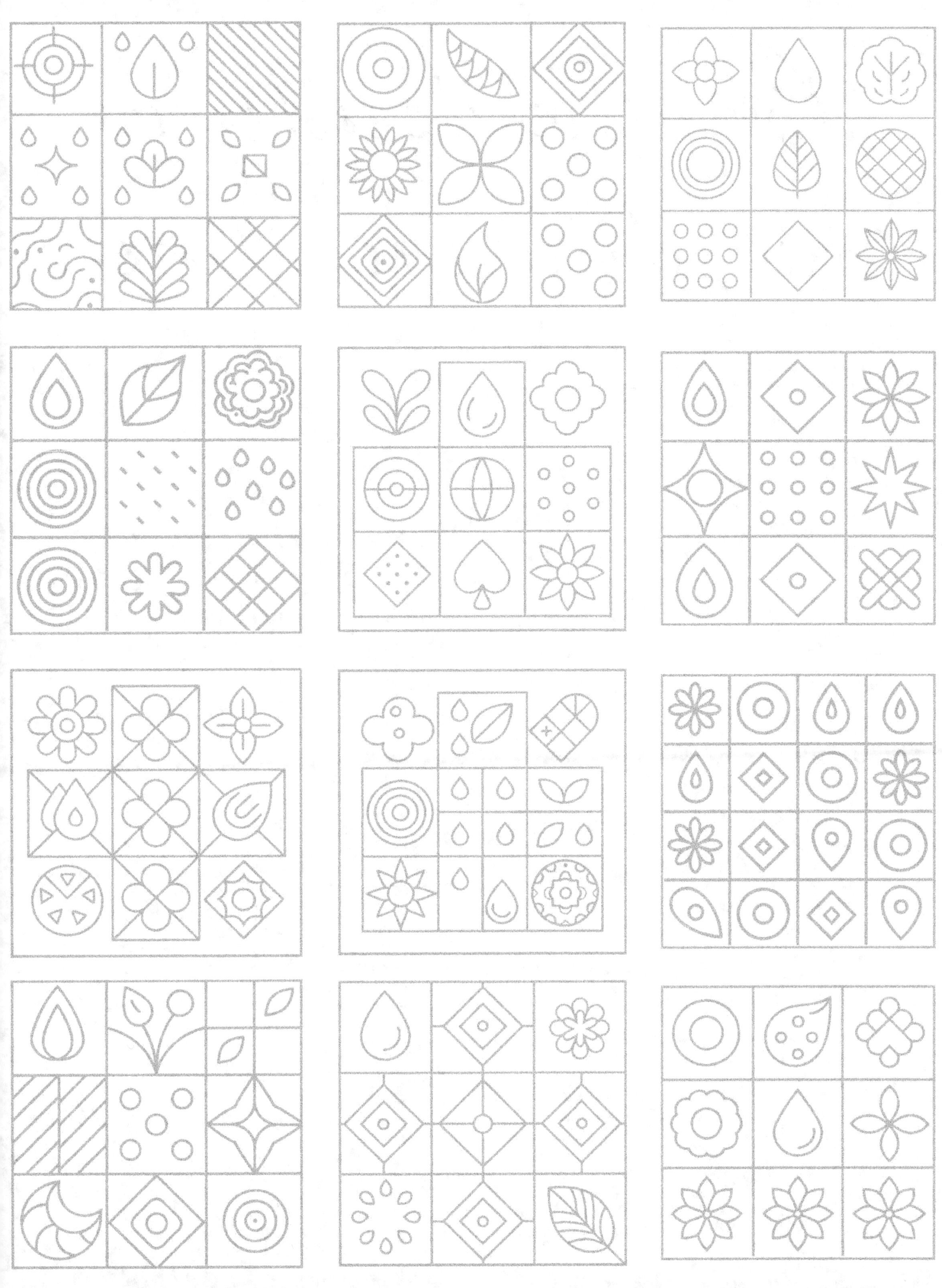

Breathe deeply as you follow each line.

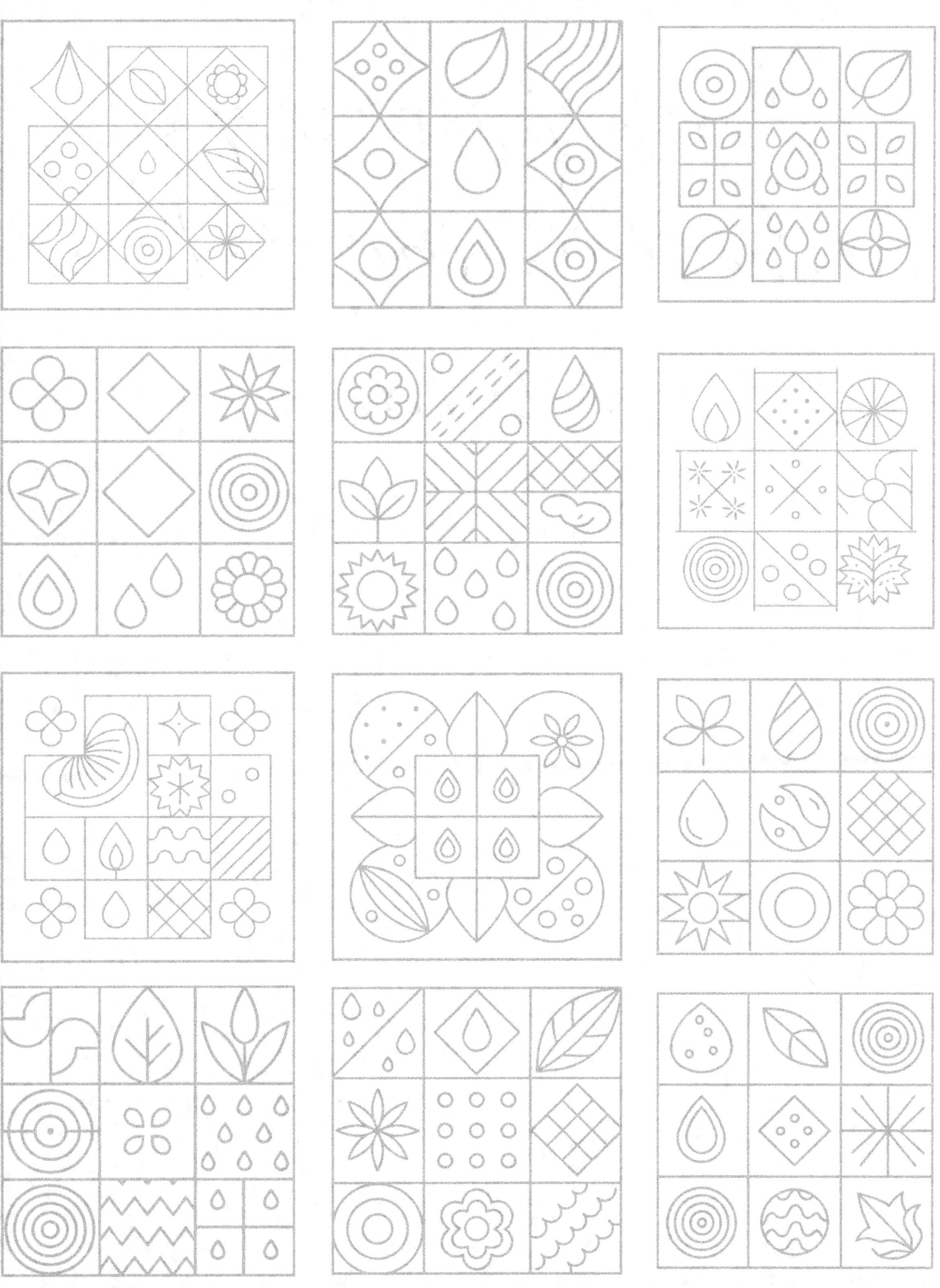

Think of tracing as meditation—one stroke at a time.

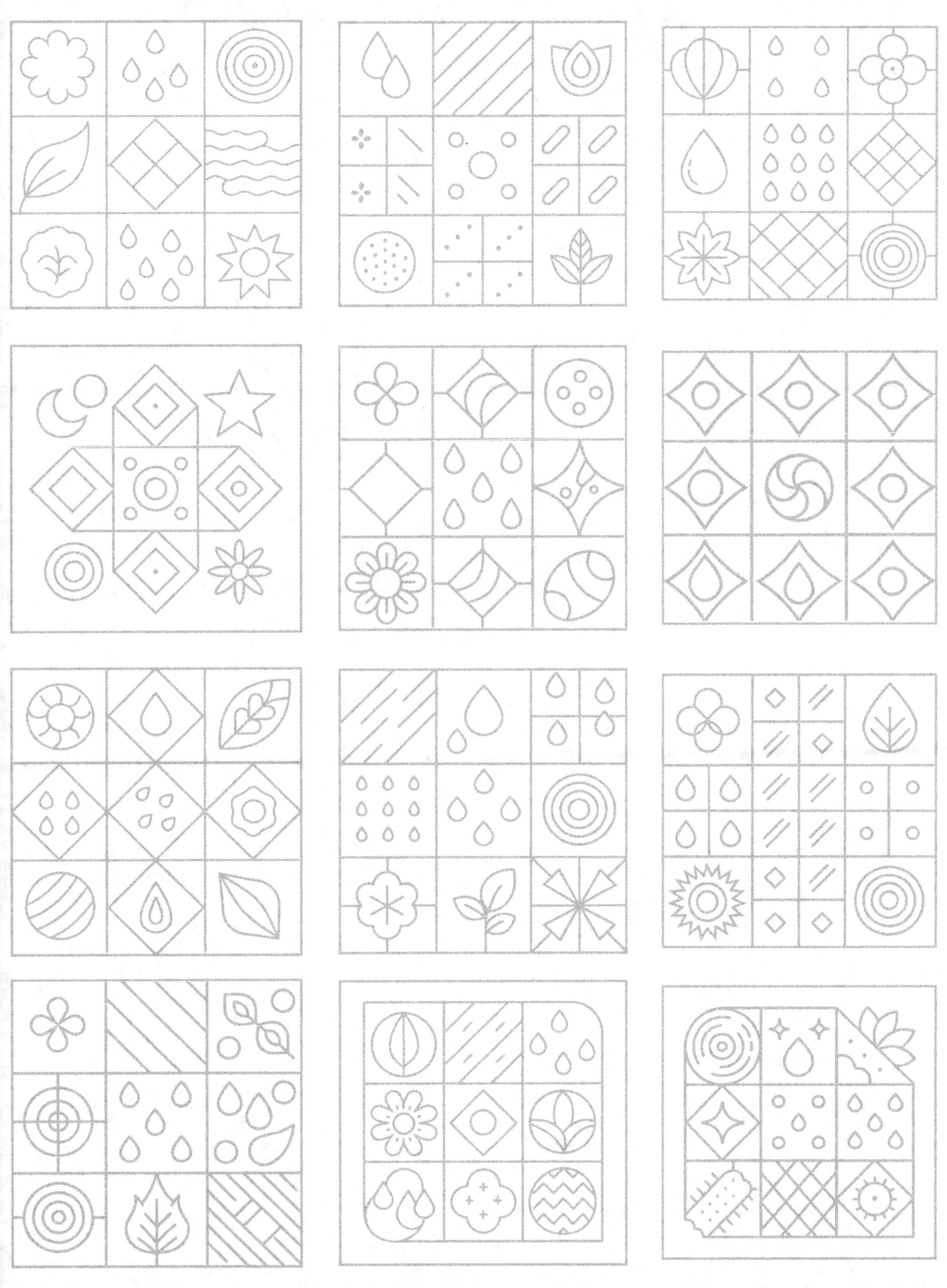

Congratulations on reaching the end of "Ink Tracing Book"! Whether you've carefully followed each line or added your own creative flair, every stroke you've made has contributed to your artistic journey. Tracing is more than just an exercise—it's a form of mindful practice, a way to refine your motor skills, and a stepping stone to creating your own unique art.

As you reflect on your progress, remember that every great artist started with simple lines. The confidence you've gained through tracing can be applied to freehand drawing, calligraphy, and even digital art. Keep experimenting, keep tracing, and most importantly—keep enjoying the process.

This book is just the beginning of your creative adventure. Whether you use it for relaxation, artistic growth, or simply the joy of drawing, I hope it has inspired you to explore more.

# We'd Love Your Feedback!

Your opinion matters! If you enjoyed this book, found it helpful, or have suggestions for improvement, I'd love to hear from you.

## How can you share your feedback?

Leave a review on the platform where you purchased this book—it helps others discover it!

Send your thoughts, suggestions, or even photos of your traced patterns to [your email or social media].

Follow us for more creative resources and future releases.

Thank you for choosing "Ink Tracing Book"—happy tracing, and may your creativity continue to flow!